Put Beginning Readers on the Right Track with
ALL ABOARD READING™

The All Aboard Reading series is especially designed for beginning readers. Written by noted authors and illustrated in full color, these are books that children really want to read—books to excite their imagination, expand their interests, make them laugh, and support their feelings. With fiction and nonfiction stories that are high interest and curriculum-related, All Aboard Reading books offer something for every young reader. And with four different reading levels, the All Aboard Reading series lets you choose which books are most appropriate for your children and their growing abilities.

Picture Readers
Picture Readers have super-simple texts, with many nouns appearing as rebus pictures. At the end of each book are 24 flash cards—on one side is a rebus picture; on the other side is the written-out word.

Station Stop 1
Station Stop 1 books are best for children who have just begun to read. Simple words and big type make these early reading experiences more comfortable. Picture clues help children to figure out the words on the page. Lots of repetition throughout the text helps children to predict the next word or phrase—an essential step in developing word recognition.

Station Stop 2
Station Stop 2 books are written specifically for children who are reading with help. Short sentences make it easier for early readers to understand what they are reading. Simple plots and simple dialogue help children with reading comprehension.

Station Stop 3
Station Stop 3 books are perfect for children who are reading alone. With longer text and harder words, these books appeal to children who have mastered basic reading skills. More complex stories captivate children who are ready for more challenging books.

In addition to All Aboard Reading books, look for All Aboard Math Readers™ (fiction stories that teach math concepts children are learning in school) and All Aboard Science Readers™ (nonfiction books that explore the most fascinating science topics in age-appropriate language).

All Aboard for happy reading!

In loving memory of my mother—K.B.J.

To my wife Vincenza—F.S.

Special thanks to Mark Ragan, Mike Scafuri, Kellen Butler, and the
Friends of the Hunley.

Scientists are finding out more about the *Hunley* all the time. Details may change, but the story
of adventure and bravery will always stay the same.

Text copyright © 2002 by Kate Boehm Jerome. Cover illustration copyright © 2002 by Bill
Farnsworth. Book illustrations copyright © 2002 by Frank Sofo. All rights reserved. Published by
Grosset & Dunlap, a division of Penguin Putnam Books for Young Readers, 345 Hudson Street,
New York, NY, 10014. ALL ABOARD READING and GROSSET & DUNLAP are trademarks of
Penguin Putnam Inc. Published simultaneously in Canada. Printed in the U.S.A.

Library of Congress Cataloging-in-Publication Data

Jerome, Kate Boehm.
Civil War sub : the mystery of the *Hunley* / by Kate Boehm Jerome ; illustrated by Frank Sofo ;
cover illustration by Bill Farnsworth.
    p. cm. – (All aboard reading. Station stop 3)
Summary: Recounts events surrounding the mysterious sinking of the Confederate submarine,
the *H.L. Hunley*, and its recent recovery from deep in the waters off the coast of South Carolina.
1. H.L. Hunley (Submarine)—Juvenile literature. 2. United States—History—Civil War, 1861-
1865—Naval operations—Submarine—Juvenile literature. 3. Submarines (Ships)—United States
—History—19th century—Juvenile literature. 4. Confederate States of America. Navy—History
—Juvenile literature. 5. Charleston (S.C.)—History—Civil War, 1861-1865—Juvenile literature.
[1. H.L. Hunley (Submarine). 2. United States—History—Civil War, 1861-1865. 3. Submarines
(Ships)—History—19th century. 4. Underwater archaeology. 5. Charleston (S.C.)—History—Civil
War, 1861-1865.]
I. Sofo, Frank, ill. II. Title. III. Series.
E599.H4 J47 2002
973.7'54—dc21
                                    2002005264

ISBN 0-448-42880-6 (GB)   A B C D E F G H I J
ISBN 0-448-42597-1 (pb)   A B C D E F G H I J

ALL ABOARD READING™

Station Stop
3

Civil War Sub
The Mystery of the Hunley

CONTRA COSTA COUNTY LIBRARY

WITHDRAWN

By Kate Boehm Jerome
Illustrated by Frank Sofo

Grosset & Dunlap • New York

Chapter One

Everyone is excited in the City of Charleston, South Carolina. It is August 8, 2000, and an old mystery is about to be solved.

Boats, loaded with people, circle around a barge. Everybody watches as a big crane works to lift a heavy load from the ocean floor. Slowly something breaks the surface of the water. The crowd holds its breath.

Then, there it is—the "mystery." It is a Civil War submarine. As it rises above the waves, the crowd cheers. The sound of boat horns fills the air. The submarine has been at the bottom of the sea for 136 years. Now it is finally coming home.

4

The submarine was named the *H.L. Hunley*. During the Civil War, it was a real secret weapon for the South. And on a cold winter night in 1864, it became the first submarine in the world to sink an enemy ship. Its target was a Northern ship called the *Housatonic*. The unlucky *Housatonic* was surprised by the attack. It sank within minutes.

The *Hunley* was unlucky, too. It should have returned to shore in victory.

But the forty-foot sub never made it back. In fact, it was never heard from again. What happened that night? Why did the *Hunley* go down after it sank the *Housatonic?*

Finding the *Hunley* may answer the questions. Now scientists can study the old submarine to see why it sank. They can also learn more about how this amazing secret weapon worked.

Chapter Two

The year is 1861.

The United States is about to break apart in the Civil War. People from Southern states want to split from the Northern states. They want to form their own country—the Confederate States of America. Most Northerners, including President Abraham Lincoln, want the country to stay together.

The two sides cannot agree on important issues. The main problem is slavery. Most Southerners want to keep slavery. They think that slaves are needed to run their huge plantations. Most Northerners think slavery is wrong.

Each side works hard to find a way

to win the war. The North has a big plan. They decide to block Southern ports with battleships. These battleships will stop European ships from delivering goods to the South.

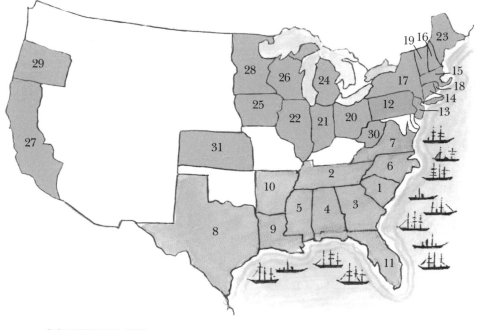

CONFEDERATE STATES

(1) South Carolina
(2) Tennessee
(3) Georgia
(4) Alabama
(5) Mississippi
(6) North Carolina
(7) Virginia
(8) Texas
(9) Louisiana
(10) Arkansas
(11) Florida

UNION STATES

(12) Pennsylvania
(13) New Jersey
(14) Connecticut
(15) Massachusetts
(16) New Hampshire
(17) New York
(18) Rhode Island
(19) Vermont
(20) Ohio
(21) Indiana
(22) Illinois

(23) Maine
(24) Michigan
(25) Iowa
(26) Wisconsin
(27) California
(28) Minnesota
(29) Oregon
(30) West Virginia
(31) Kansas

Two men from the South hatch a bold plan. James McClintock and Baxter Watson decide to try to build a submarine—an underwater battleship. A submarine could sink Northern battleships. Then supply ships will be able to land once again. Another man is interested in the project. His name is Captain Horace L. Hunley. He decides to give his time and his money to the effort.

McClintock, Watson, and Hunley build their first test sub in New Orleans. But they are forced to sink it when the North invades the harbor. Another test sub sinks in Alabama. Money is running out. Luckily, a group of rich Southern men come to the rescue. They help Captain Hunley pay the bills. The total cost of a new submarine is $15,000. That is a lot of money in 1863!

The new model is a beauty. The men use metal strips to widen a long metal boiler. They make both ends curve toward a point. This makes a tube forty feet long, three-and-a-half feet wide, and four feet deep. At each end of the tube they put a water tank. These tanks will be used to allow the boat to sink beneath the water.

The group decides to name the submarine after Captain H.L. Hunley, the man who has spent so much time and money on it. The *Hunley* is an amazing machine. It holds seven crewmen and their captain. They must enter through two sixteen-inch hatches. When they are in position, the men can not move more than a foot. They can't even stand up. Once the hatches are closed, the crew has only the air that is trapped inside. When that air is gone, they must go above water and open the hatches again. If they do not get more air in time, they will die.

Even though the *Hunley* has no engine, it can go pretty fast underwater. How? The crewmen use all their strength to push and pull on a crank. The crank turns a propeller that powers the boat. It is the captain's job to steer the submarine. This job is very important. Everyone's life is in the captain's hands.

Chapter Three

While the *Hunley* is being tested, the Southern port of Charleston, South Carolina, falls into big trouble. Northern ships block the harbor. Supplies cannot get to the Southern troops; the city is running short of what it needs. If Charleston surrenders to the North, it will be a big loss for the South.

Two of the men working on the *Hunley* decide to visit Charleston's military commander. General Pierre Gustave Toutant Beauregard knows he needs help. And he is famous for liking rather odd ideas. When he hears about the strange underwater machine, he is excited. General Beauregard wants the *Hunley*

moved to the harbor near Charleston. Once there, it can get ready for a sneak attack on nearby enemy ships.

In August of 1863, the *Hunley* is tied to two railroad flatcars to begin its journey to Charleston. It is hard to keep the little submarine a secret. Everybody who sees it wants to know what it is. To hide it, the men cover the submarine with big cloths.

When the *Hunley* reaches Charleston, the city comes alive with excitement. Will this be the secret weapon that defeats the dreaded Northern fleet?

Every day things get worse for Charleston. Early in the morning of August 22, the Northern troops aim a huge cannon at the city. It is nicknamed "The Swamp Angel." The cannon's shells travel a long way and explode all over Charleston's streets. Some days more than one hundred shells are let loose. People keep tubs of water all around. They never know when they will need the water to put out a fire.

The crew that works the *Hunley* practices hard. The military leaders want the submarine to attack right away. But the crew of the *Hunley* thinks they need more practice. It is not easy to steer the sub through the tides. The crew says it is not ready to make an attack.

The Confederate Navy is losing patience. A new man is put in charge. Lieutenant John Payne heads a new crew. Lt. Payne wastes no time learning how to

pilot the tiny sub. Some worry that he is not taking enough time.

On August 29, as the crew practices diving and coming back up, disaster strikes. The *Hunley* accidentally goes underwater with its hatches still open. Lt. Payne and another man scramble to safety. Another crewman is dragged forty feet underwater but manages to escape. Five other men are not so lucky. They are trapped in the submarine and drown.

Even though the *Hunley* is stuck more than forty feet below the surface of the water, she is raised. This is a very difficult job. But divers finally bring the submarine back up. The five dead crewmen are recovered and buried.

Soon the submarine is practicing dives again. On the morning of October 15, 1863, the new crew heads out for a

test run. Horace Hunley leads the crew. The
dive starts out well. But then something
goes terribly wrong. The submarine never
comes back up. After an agonizing time,
everyone realizes the crew, including H.L.
Hunley himself, has drowned.

General Beauregard is very discour-
aged. He gives up on the submarine. He
feels that the ship is more dangerous

to its crews than to the enemy. The submarine was supposed to save Charleston; now its nickname is the "murderous machine."

However, one man still believes in the *Hunley*. Lt. George Dixon is a brave soldier who has an interesting battle history. He walks with a limp. At a famous Civil War battle he was struck by enemy fire. Amazingly, a gold coin in his pocket stopped the bullet from killing him. His girlfriend had given him the gold coin. Some people say that he now carries it with him everywhere. It is his good luck charm.

Chapter Four

Lt. George Dixon is a very brave man. He will not give up on the *Hunley*. He convinces General Beauregard to let him take command of the submarine for one more try.

The *Hunley* sits on the bottom of the ocean for a couple weeks before the salvage crew can get her up. When she is raised, the eight unlucky crew members are buried with military honors. The *Hunley* floats in the water for another few months. Lt. Dixon wants to make repairs and re-equip the tiny submarine for the dangerous journey ahead.

Finally, once again the *Hunley* is ready. Lt. Dixon asks for another crew.

Amazingly, more men volunteer. Even though the sailors know that thirteen men have already died on the sub, they want the honor of serving on the *Hunley*.

The new crew practices day after day. The job is very tiring. The men have to hike seven miles to the bay where the *Hunley* is docked. Then they squeeze into the tiny sub and drill for several hours. After a rest and dinner, the men get back into the sub. Under the cover of darkness they take the *Hunley* out into the ocean.

It is cold and dark. And the men never know if the enemy will spot them

when the sub comes up for more air.
They turn the hand crank for hours and
hours. They get very sore and tired.
Sometimes they go six or seven miles
away from shore.

By dawn the men are back in port
with a seven-mile march back to their
camps. After a few hours of sleep, the
crew must be ready to start all over.

In late January of 1864, the crew gets a break. Lt. Dixon moves his men closer to the *Hunley*. Now, at least, they won't have to make such a long hike every day.

The Northern fleet once again hears reports of the underwater attack ship. The North keeps its iron warships, called "ironclads," close to shore. They feel the ironclads are strong enough to withstand any attack. But they aren't so sure about their wooden ships. They move them farther from shore. They figure that the *Hunley* can't go that far out to sea.

Around mid-February, 1864, a new Northern warship is seen around Charleston. The *Housatonic* is a fast wooden boat. It chases any ships trying to break the blockade. At night it drops anchor only a few miles offshore from where the *Hunley* is docked.

Lt. Dixon has been waiting for a break like this. He knows the *Housatonic* is close enough for the *Hunley* to attack. But there's a problem. The winter wind is whipping up the ocean waves. The water is too rough to take the *Hunley* out to sea. The crew waits. They need just one night of clear weather. Finally, on February 17, 1864, the big waves flatten out.

Now is their chance.

After sunset, Dixon and his men climb into the submarine. They know the plan by heart. They will sneak up on the *Housatonic*. Then they will ram the wooden ship with a long iron pole that is attached to the front of the sub. At the end of the pole is a torpedo. (A torpedo is like a huge bullet that explodes.) The *Hunley* will leave the torpedo in the wooden ship. Then, once the *Hunley* gets 150 yards away, a

The crew cranks for more than an hour. Dixon knows the sub must be close to the *Housatonic*. But he has to be sure. The hatch is cracked open. There, less than a mile ahead, lies the *Housatonic!*

The *Hunley* proceeds with her attack. However, a lookout on the *Housatonic* sees something. The crew on the *Housatonic* begins firing bullets at the *Hunley*. But its iron hull is strong, and the *Hunley* stays steady in her attack.

rope on the outside of the sub will pull
the trigger on the torpedo. The torpedo
will explode and the *Housatonic* will go
down. At least that is the plan. If all goes
well, the *Hunley* will shine a blue light.
That is the signal to shore—mission
accomplished.

Within seconds the *Hunley* hits the *Housatonic*. Its iron pole jabs the ship and puts the torpedo in place. Quickly, Lt. Dixon orders the *Hunley* to back away.

The rope trips the trigger. The torpedo explodes. Shock waves hit both the sub and the wooden ship. A big hole is ripped in the *Housatonic*. Water floods into the ship. The panicked crew rushes to the deck. The *Housatonic* is rolling onto its side. The wooden ship is going down.

Men scramble into lifeboats. Some cling to the sails still above water. It takes less than five minutes for the *Housatonic* to sink. Another Northern ship comes to rescue men from the water. But five *Housatonic* sailors drown.

As for the *Hunley*, what happened? That night it made history. It was the first submarine to sink an enemy ship. Some on shore say that the *Hunley* crew flashed a blue light for victory. But the *Hunley* never made it back to its dock. On that cold night in February, the famous secret weapon and all of her crew sank to the bottom of the ocean.

A little more than a year later, the Civil War ends. On April 9, 1865, General Robert E. Lee surrenders his Southern troops to General Ulysses S. Grant of the North. The United States will fly one flag again. Slavery will end.

After a while not many people remember the *Hunley*. The sub didn't change the course of the war for the South. Still, it did accomplish its purpose. The brave men of the *Hunley* proved that submarine warfare was possible. Within fifty years, submarines were used in naval battles all over the world.

Chapter Five

Although everyone knew the *Hunley* was gone, nobody knew exactly where the sub went down. Some thought the tide had carried the sub out to sea. Others thought it might have broken into pieces and been washed away. But many thought that the boat was still on the bottom, perhaps close to where the *Housatonic* sank.

More than one hundred years pass. People still tell stories about the *Hunley*. One of those storytellers falls in love with the idea of finding the sunken treasure. His name is Clive Cussler. He's an author of adventure stories. Finding the *Hunley* will be a real-life adventure.

Cussler spends fifteen years searching for the *Hunley*. Finally, on May 3, 1995, the great discovery is made. In thirty feet of water and just about four miles from shore, the *Hunley* is found. It is buried in mud. And it is still in one piece!

It takes four more years to figure out
how to bring up the *Hunley*. A team of
scientists from all over the world gets
together with underwater experts. They
finally agree on a plan.

By 1999, the scientists and divers are
working hard in the ocean around the
Hunley. They build a huge platform. Then
a big crane is carried out. The *Hunley* is
resting on one side. Scientists know they
will have to keep it on its side when they
bring it up. Otherwise, every thing inside

the sub could shift and the sub might break apart.

So how will they do this? The experts design a hammock to put under the *Hunley*. Sand is cleared away beneath the sub. The work is slow because the divers can hardly see in the dark water. Stinging jellyfish are also a problem. But finally the slings of the hammock go under the sub. Next, foam is pumped into bags attached to the slings. The foam hardens to keep the *Hunley* on its side.

On August 8, 2000, the big crane brings the *Hunley* out of the water. It is set down gently on a barge that will take it to a research lab. Cheers go up as hundreds of boats escort the *Hunley* back to port. Clive Cussler is among those cheering. He can hardly believe that his real-life adventure is coming to a successful end.

Thousands of people line the bridges and docks to welcome the *Hunley* home. Church bells ring in the city. They ring to honor both the Northern and Southern soldiers who lost their lives in the 1864 sea battle. They ring to honor a country still strong and still united.

Chapter 6

The *Hunley* is safely at rest in a research tank built just for it. The water in the tank is kept below forty-six degrees. This slows the growth of any harmful bacteria. It's important to keep the *Hunley* underwater. Air is its worst enemy. This is because oxygen in the air can rust the old metal of the submarine.

Although scientists will study the *Hunley* for years, they are already amazed at what they've found. After months of work, some parts of the submarine are removed so scientists can look inside. Using hand tools and buckets, the researchers slowly scrape through all the mud. A canteen, the bottom of a wax candle, a pencil, and other items are found. Ordinary items back then, but so special to us now. All these things were used by the *Hunley's* crew. Now they will help scientists piece together a story of life aboard the sub.

But the researchers' most important find is the skeletons of all eight men. This includes the remains of Lt. George Dixon, the brave captain of the submarine. And do you know what was near Lt. Dixon? His lucky gold coin. It was the same gold piece that stopped the bullet and saved his life at the Battle of Shiloh. So the legend was true. Lt. Dixon did carry the coin with him as a good luck charm. The proof is on the back of the coin itself. Lt. Dixon had engraved it.

So what did happen on that cold February night in 1864 when the *Hunley* sank to the bottom of the sea? At first researchers guessed that a bullet fired from the *Housatonic* may have broken the captain's glass lookout tower. If a bullet had hit Captain Dixon, the sub would have been out of control with water leaking inside. But wouldn't others in the crew have taken over the controls?

Wouldn't the sailors have tried to escape through the hatches?

Now that the sub is open, the researchers are beginning to find some answers. All of the soldiers' bodies were at their posts. It doesn't look like there was any struggle or panic. It may be that the men simply ran out of air. If this is what happened, they would have fallen asleep and met a peaceful death.

In fact, the full story may never be known. There is still much to learn as scientists continue their slow and careful study. Even though the sub was underwater for so long, it is still in good shape. Scientists are hopeful that they will find many more personal belongings of the soldiers. These rare finds could tell us much more about the men and the lives they led. And what a rich history present that would be from the brave crew of the *Hunley!*